Maya Lin

THINKING WITH HER HANDS

By Susan Goldman Rubin

chronicle books · san francisco

For my daughter Katherine.

Jacket/case images, front (clockwise from top left): Maya Lin drawing *Eleven Minute Line*, Anders
Norsell. Courtesy of The Wanås Foundation; Photo of Maya Lin © 2006 by AP Photo/Jackie Johnston;
Riggio-Lynch Chapel, Timothy Hursley. Courtesy Maya Lin Studio; Young child visiting the Vietnam
Veterans Memorial © Mickie DeVries/Offset.com.
Jacket/case image, back: Drawing from Maya Lin's submission for the Vietnam Veterans Memorial.
Library of Congress.
Endpaper images: Drawings from Maya Lin's submission for the Vietnam Veterans Memorial.
Library of Congress.
Additional image credits and copyright information on p. 97.

Library of Congress Cataloging-in-Publication Data:

Names: Rubin, Susan Goldman, author.
Title: Maya Lin : thinking with her hands / Susan Rubin.
Description: San Francisco : Chronicle Books, 2017.
Identifiers: LCCN 2016058584 | ISBN 9781452108377 (hardback)
Subjects: LCSH: Lin, Maya Ying—Juvenile literature. | Architects—United States—Biography—Juvenile
literature. | Chinese American architects—United States—Biography—Juvenile literature. | Artists—
United States—Biography—Juvenile literature. | Chinese American artists—United States—Biography—
Juvenile literature. | BISAC: JUVENILE NONFICTION / Biography & Autobiography / Art. | JUVENILE
NONFICTION / History / United States / 20th Century. | JUVENILE NONFICTION / Art / General.
Classification: LCC NA737.L48 R83 2017 | DDC 720.92 [B] —dc23 LC record available at https://lccn.loc
.gov/2016058584

Manufactured in China.

Design by Kayla Ferriera.
Typeset in Pluto Sans, Silica, and Bryant Pro.

10 9 8 7 6 5 4 3 2 1

Chronicle Books LLC
680 Second Street
San Francisco, California 94107

Chronicle Books—we see things differently.
Become part of our community at www.chroniclekids.com.

Contents

Why write a book about Maya Lin? I wanted to find out more about the woman who designed one of the most visited memorials in the world, the Vietnam Veterans Memorial in Washington, D.C., while she was still just a college student. As I did research, I discovered other works she had designed that deeply moved me: the Civil Rights Memorial in Montgomery, Alabama; the Langston Hughes Library and Riggio-Lynch Interfaith Chapel in Clinton, Tennessee; and the memorial that she is currently working on, which she says will be her last. Titled *What Is Missing?*, it is a science-based project intended to make people aware of species and habitat loss around the world.

But Maya does not want to be known only for her memorials. She says, "You need to see me whole as an artist. What I'm doing is art, architecture, *and* memorials."

In this book I hope I have achieved that goal and have captured the artist Maya Lin thinking with her hands.

"I was making things my whole childhood and I still am."

Maya Lin

Clay

CHAPTER ONE: Cable Lane

As a child Maya never dreamed of becoming an artist. She loved animals and planned to become a veterinarian when she grew up. She and her older brother, Tan, roamed the woods behind their house on Cable Lane in Athens, Ohio. She would sit quietly and watch the rabbits, squirrels, and birds. Maya didn't have many friends. "So I made up my own world," she says. In her bedroom she built paper houses and villages, and later she made things out of silver and clay. All these childhood experiences were to greatly influence her adult work as an artist and architect.

Maya Ying Lin was born on October 5, 1959. Her middle name means "precious stone" in Chinese. She and Tan grew up surrounded by art. "My father was a ceramicist and my mother a poet," wrote Maya. Her parents both taught at Ohio University.

Maya, around age four, Athens, Ohio.

Every afternoon after school she and Tan walked over to their father's studio. Maya loved to watch her father knead the clay, pound it, push it, and cut it through with wire. "He worked with it effortlessly," she wrote. Maya's father would let her play with clay. At home the family ate from stoneware plates and bowls that he had made. The glazes on the ceramics were the natural earth colors that Maya liked best—and still does.

Her mother, on the other hand, preferred red, the color that in Chinese tradition symbolizes good luck and happiness. Maya said, "My mother dressed me up in too many red dresses. I hate the color red!"

Maya's parents had both been born in China. They had escaped to the United States in the 1940s during a civil war. From an early age Maya was very aware of her parents' feeling that Athens, Ohio, was not really home. "For them, their true home, China, belonged to the past," she wrote. Yet they didn't talk about their history, and Maya didn't ask questions. She didn't know her grandparents or her aunts and uncles. "When I was little," she said, "we would get letters from China, in Chinese, and they'd be censored."

● Maya, around age one, with her brother, Tan, and their parents in their home in Athens, Ohio.

Although Maya says she comes from "two heritages," she didn't think of herself as Asian American as she was growing up. "I thought I was white. I wanted to fit in," she said.

> " I probably spent the first twenty years of my life wanting to be as American as possible. "

Maya loved school. "I studied like crazy," she said. "I was a Class A nerd." While she was still a student in Athens High School, she took courses in computers and science at the university. She got straight As in everything except for one subject: gym. She despised it and failed.

In most classes Maya wound up as teacher's pet. As a result, she says, "the other kids probably hated me. I didn't have any friends." Instead she enjoyed hanging out with her teachers. She and her chemistry teacher, Miss McCallan, stayed after school and did experiments. "One time I made this incredible powder, flash powder, and I made way too much of it," recalled Maya gleefully. "And it exploded!" The sound the explosion made was so loud that Maya and Miss McCallan temporarily went deaf. The head science teacher stormed in and said, "What did I just hear?" The two culprits said innocently, "Nothing. We didn't hear anything."

Maya didn't fit in at high school. She wore no makeup and didn't date. Her long hair fell down to her knees. She looked younger than kids her age. "I was the smallest in my class," she recalled. "I was half the weight of everyone else."

She and her brother stayed close to home. "We always ate dinner with our parents," she said. "We weren't going to the proms or going to the football games."

By her senior year Maya was counting the days till she could leave Athens and go to college. On a lark she applied to Yale, an Ivy League school, never thinking she'd get in. No student from Athens High School had ever gone there. But to Maya's surprise she was accepted. So in the fall of 1977 she eagerly took off for New Haven, Connecticut.

Granite

CHAPTER TWO: The Vietnam Veterans Memorial

When Maya arrived at Yale she was shocked to find that she felt like "the dumbest" person in her class. "It was very, very intimidating," she said. Then she began making friends with classmates and professors and felt more at home. "For the first time I felt that I fit in."

Maya had planned on becoming a field zoologist. But when her science advisor told her that Yale's animal behavior program required dissecting live animals she quickly changed her mind. Instead, she chose architecture. "It was this perfect combination of art and math, art and science."

In her senior year Maya worked with a group of students to study funereal architecture for their senior project. They were learning about tombs and other memorials built to remember the dead. One of the students saw

Visitors of all ages are moved by the power of the memorial and often respond by touching the names of veterans who lost their lives in the war.

a bulletin posted at the architecture school announcing a competition to design a Vietnam Veterans Memorial in Washington, D.C. The class decided to make designs for the contest simply as an exercise.

Maya had been just a young girl during the years of the controversial war, and like many children her age she was not very "news-conscious." But when she started to think about the memorial, instead of researching the war's history and the conflict of political views about it, she asked herself basic questions: "What exactly is a memorial? What should it do?" She said,

" I try to understand the 'why' of a project before it's a 'what.' "

She also looked at pictures of earlier war memorials. "Many of these . . . included the names of those killed," she said. "They captured what I felt memorials should be: honest about the reality of war, about the loss of life in war, and about remembering those who served and especially those who died." A memorial that particularly impressed her is located in Thiepval, France. It includes

● Maya's self-portrait, senior year at Yale University.

more than seventy-two thousand names honoring British and South African soldiers who were listed as missing in World War I.

Maya was also deeply moved by a memorial in Woolsey Hall at Yale that was inscribed with the names of alumni killed in wars. "I had never been able to resist touching the names cut into these marble walls," she wrote.

One of the contest requirements for the Vietnam Memorial was to incorporate the fifty-seven thousand names of those missing and killed. Looking at the names, thought Maya, would enable people to "respond and remember."

She and a few of her classmates went to Washington to see the proposed location for the memorial. The site was a beautiful park on the Mall between the Washington Monument and the Lincoln Memorial. "At the site the idea for the design took shape," she wrote. "I had a simple impulse to cut into the earth."

Maya envisioned flat, mirrored surfaces emerging from the ground, so she chose black granite, which, when polished, is highly reflective. The names of those killed and missing would be carved on two walls shaped like the

One section of the Vietnam Veterans Memorial points toward the Washington Monument.

letter V. One wall would point to the Lincoln Memorial, the other to the Washington Monument. Maya said,

"I wanted to create a unity between the nation's past and present."

Back at Yale she quickly sketched her idea. "It almost seemed too simple, too little," she wrote. She shaped the first model out of mashed potatoes in the dining hall. Then she modeled the form out of Plasticine, a clay material. "I think with my hands," she wrote. "My brother and I played with clay our entire childhoods." So developing her design in clay seemed completely natural.

Maya's professor thought her Plasticine model painted glossy black was "eccentric." And he criticized her plan to list the names in chronological order, beginning on the left panel and continuing on the right. He said that the apex, the point where the walls met, should be more important. Maya felt strongly about the order of the names, but she could see her professor's meaning. So she changed

● Maya's submission for the Vietnam Veterans Memorial project was number 1026, and one of the last to come in.

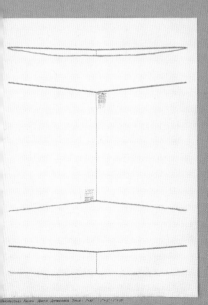

IN MEMORIAM

Walking through this park-like area, the memorial appears as a rift in the earth—a long, polished black stone wall, emerging from and receding into the earth. Approaching the memorial, the ground slopes gently downward, and the low walls emerging on either side, growing out of the earth, extend and converge at a point below and ahead. Walking into the grassy site contained by the walls of this memorial we can barely make out the carved names upon the memorial's walls. These names, seemingly infinite in number, convey the sense of overwhelming numbers, while unifying these individuals into a whole. For this memorial is meant not as a monument to the individual, but rather as a memorial to the men and women who died during this war, as a whole.

The memorial is composed not as an unchanging monument, but as a moving composition, to be understood as we move into and out of it; the passage itself is gradual, the descent to the origin slow, but it is at the origin that the meaning of this memorial is to fully understood. At the intersection of these walls, on the right side, at this wall's top is carved the date of the first death. It is followed by the names of those who have died in the war, in chronological order. These names continue on this wall, appearing to recede into the earth at the wall's end. The names resume on the left wall, as the wall emerges from the earth, continuing back to the origin, where the date of the last death is carved, at the bottom of this wall. Thus the war's beginning and end meet; the war is "complete", coming full circle, yet broken by the earth that bounds the angle's open side, and contained within the earth itself. As we turn to leave, we see these walls stretching into the distance, directing us to the Washington Monument to the left and the Lincoln Memorial to the right, thus bringing the Vietnam Memorial into historical context. We, the living are brought to a concrete realization of these deaths.

Brought to a sharp awareness of such a loss, it is up to each individual to resolve or come to terms with this loss. For death is in the end a personal and private matter, and the area contained within this memorial is a quiet place meant for personal reflection and private reckoning. The black granite walls, each 200 feet long, and 10 feet below ground at their lowest point (gradually ascending towards ground level) effectively act as a sound barrier, yet are of such a height and length so as not to appear threatening or enclosing. The actual area is wide and shallow; allowing for a sense of privacy and the sunlight from the memorial's southern exposure along with the grassy park surrounding and within it's wall contribute to the serenity of the area. Thus this memorial is for these who have died, and for us to remember them.

The memorial's origin is located approximately at the center of this site; it legs each extending 200 feet towards the Washington Monument and the Lincoln Memorial. The walls, contained on one side by the earth is are 10 feet below ground at their point of origin, gradually lessening in height, until they finally recede totally into the earth at their ends. The walls are to be made of a hard, polished black granite, with the names to be carved in a simple Trojan letter, 3/4 inch high, allowing for nine inches in length for each name. The memorial's construction involves recontouring the area within the wall's boundaries so as to provide for an easily accessible descent, but as much of the site as possible should be left untouched (including trees). The area should be made into a park for all the public to enjoy.

her design so that the names begin and end at the apex, connecting the beginning of the war to the end.

Maya and her professor were the only ones in the class who submitted their entries. As part of her submission Maya wrote a one-page description of her design. She wrote the essay by hand and kept revising it up to the last minute. The deadline was March 31, 1981. "It took longer . . . to write the statement . . . than to design the memorial," she said. Maya sent off her project, never expecting to hear about it again.

On the last day of classes there was a phone call from Washington. Someone from the Vietnam Veterans Memorial Fund wanted to speak to her. Maya hurried to take the call and learned that three people from the fund were coming up to Yale to see her. She thought they were going to ask her technical questions about her design. "It never occurred to me that I might have won the competition," she wrote. "It was still, in my mind, an exercise."

So Maya was calm as the officers from the fund met with her in her dorm room and told her the startling news. Out of 1,421 entries, her design had won the contest. She

Maya wrote her one-page essay freehand and kept rewording the description up to the very last minute.

was stunned. "I think my roommate's face showed more emotion than mine did," she said.

As a young woman with an Asian name, Maya knew that she probably was not what the judges of the competition expected. Despite her win, her professor gave her only a B-plus for the class.

> "I often wondered, if it had not been an anonymous entry . . . would I have been selected?"

On the day she graduated from Yale, Maya moved to Washington, D.C., to be a consultant on the project. "I immediately became part of an internal struggle for control of the design," she wrote. "I think my age made it seem apparent to some that I was too young to understand what I had done or to see it through to completion." She doubted that her design would ever be built.

One of the concerns continued to be how to list the names. Some people felt that they should be listed alphabetically. But when they realized that more than

Maya displaying her model for the Vietnam Veterans Memorial at a press conference held by the Vietnam Veterans Memorial Fund in Washington, D.C., in 1981.

six hundred Smiths had died in the war, they knew it was not a good idea. Maya said, "I fought hard to maintain the chronological listing." She wanted veterans to find the names of fallen soldiers they had served with grouped together. She placed symbols beside each name indicating that a soldier had died, was missing in action, or a prisoner of war. She also devised a way to alter the symbol if a missing veteran later returned alive.

Controversy arose over her choice of black granite. One of the architects thought the polished surface was "too *feminine*." Some veterans objected to black because it was a color of "shame and dishonor." They wanted the memorial to be white. Maya explained that she thought of polished black granite as "a dark mirror" giving people an "interface between the world of the living and the world of the dead."

At a meeting of the Commission of Fine Arts, a government agency that was to approve the final design, there were heated discussions. One angry veteran complained that Maya's design was "a black scar," and he asked for the competition to be reopened. Ross Perot, a billionaire who had contributed money for the competition, withdrew his support. He criticized Maya's memorial as "inappropriate" and said it looked like a wound in the earth. He asked Maya if she didn't agree that the "veterans would prefer . . . something happy and uplifting."

Others said that her V-shaped design was secretly meant to be a peace sign signifying her opposition to the war. Many veterans proposed that a statue of three infantrymen be placed in the center of the memorial. Maya vehemently objected, believing that a realistic statue would "violate that private contemplative space."

The debates continued as newspapers and government officials attacked her for being a woman, and so young. Most hurtful to Maya were racist comments about her being Asian. Some people felt that a memorial for a war that had been fought against Asians should not be designed by someone of Asian heritage. Although Maya's parents had come from China, she had been born and raised in Ohio. "I was as American as anyone else," she wrote.

Maya defended herself on TV and at press conferences. After a miserable year sitting through tense subcommittee hearings, she left Washington and missed the groundbreaking, the first day of construction. "I wanted to pretend it never happened," she said. "I tried to forget it." Maya moved to Boston and studied at the Harvard Graduate School of Design and then worked for an archi-tectural firm.

When she returned to Washington for the dedication, the granite panels were already up."It was a strange feel-ing, to have had an idea that was solely yours be no longer a part of your mind but totally public," she wrote.

The memorial was dedicated on November 13, 1982.

Two years later, despite Maya's objection, a bronze statue of three Vietnam soldiers, one black, one white, and one Latino, by sculptor Frederick Hart, was added. The slightly larger-than-life sculpture was placed a distance away as a compromise.

Maya has said, "The first time I visited the memorial after it was completed I found myself searching out the name of a friend's father and touching it. It was strange to realize that I was another visitor and I was reacting to it as I had designed it."

New names are added each year as Vietnam veterans die of wounds and illnesses suffered during the war. There

A crowd of 150,000 people gathered at the memorial, also known as the Wall, on dedication day, November 13, 1982.

are now more than fifty-eight thousand names. They are listed in roughly chronological order, day by day by day.

The Vietnam Memorial is one of the most visited sites in the National Park Service. Veterans come to find the names of their fellow soldiers. Families of those lost in the war look for the names of their loved ones. Students leave poetry and artwork as remembrances. Sometimes they make rubbings of a soldier's name to better understand the history of the war and to learn about the memorial itself. Maya said about the memorial,

> "It's not meant to be cheerful or happy, but to bring out in people the realization of loss and a . . . healing process."

● Students from around the country and the world are among the three million people who visit the Wall every year and leave remembrances to honor the fallen soldiers.

Water

CHAPTER THREE: The Civil Rights Memorial

After the attention she received for the Vietnam Veterans Memorial, Maya was deluged with offers to design memorials. She turned them all down.

Then one day early in 1988, Maya received a phone call from Eddie Ashforth at the Southern Poverty Law Center (SPLC) in Montgomery, Alabama. The SPLC defends the rights of minorities and teaches tolerance. Since Maya's phone number was unlisted, Mr. Ashforth had called every person named M. Lin in the Manhattan phone book until he reached her. He asked if she would consider designing a memorial in remembrance of those who had died in the struggle for civil rights. "Absolutely not," thought Maya. "I did not want to be typecast as a monument designer."

But when Mr. Ashforth told her that there wasn't a national civil rights memorial, she became interested.

The water on the top of the table of the Civil Rights Memorial appears still until a visitor interacts with it by touching the surface.

"I knew very little about the civil rights movement," she wrote. Before meeting with the SPLC in Montgomery, she spent three months reading books and viewing the documentary films the SPLC sent to her. "I was shocked by what I learned," she wrote. "I was even more disturbed that the information I was learning about our history—events that were going on while I was growing up—was never taught to me in school."

The directors of the Center told her that they envisioned a stone marker at the entrance to their building listing the names of adults and children killed in the civil rights movement. Maya knew this wouldn't be enough. There were many people like her who did not really know the details of the civil rights movement in the United States. She said,

> " I realized I had to give people an understanding of what that time period was about. "

On the plane flying to Montgomery for her first meeting at the Center, she read Dr. Martin Luther King Jr.'s famous "I Have a Dream" speech. She was struck by his words, especially these adapted from the Bible: "We are not satisfied, and we will not be satisfied until justice rolls down like waters and righteousness like a mighty stream."

"Immediately I knew that the memorial would be about water," she wrote. Maya sketched her idea on a napkin. There would be a curved wall with part of Dr. King's quote engraved on it. Water would spill down the face of the wall. Later she thought that below the wall, a circular stone sculpture resembling a sundial or flat table would contain a timeline of the civil rights movement and the victims' names. Water would emerge gently from the middle of the sculpture and flow evenly across the top. She showed her design to the SPLC group and they approved.

Back in New York she began to make models and drawings to refine her idea. Asymmetry was to be an important feature. The circular water table would be placed to the side of the wall, not directly in the center of it. Maya said, "I am conveying a simple conceptual message—things don't have to be or look identical in order to be balanced or equal."

...UNTIL JUSTICE RO

AND RIGHTEOUSNES

- The Civil Rights Memorial is inscribed with
a quote from Dr. Martin Luther King Jr.

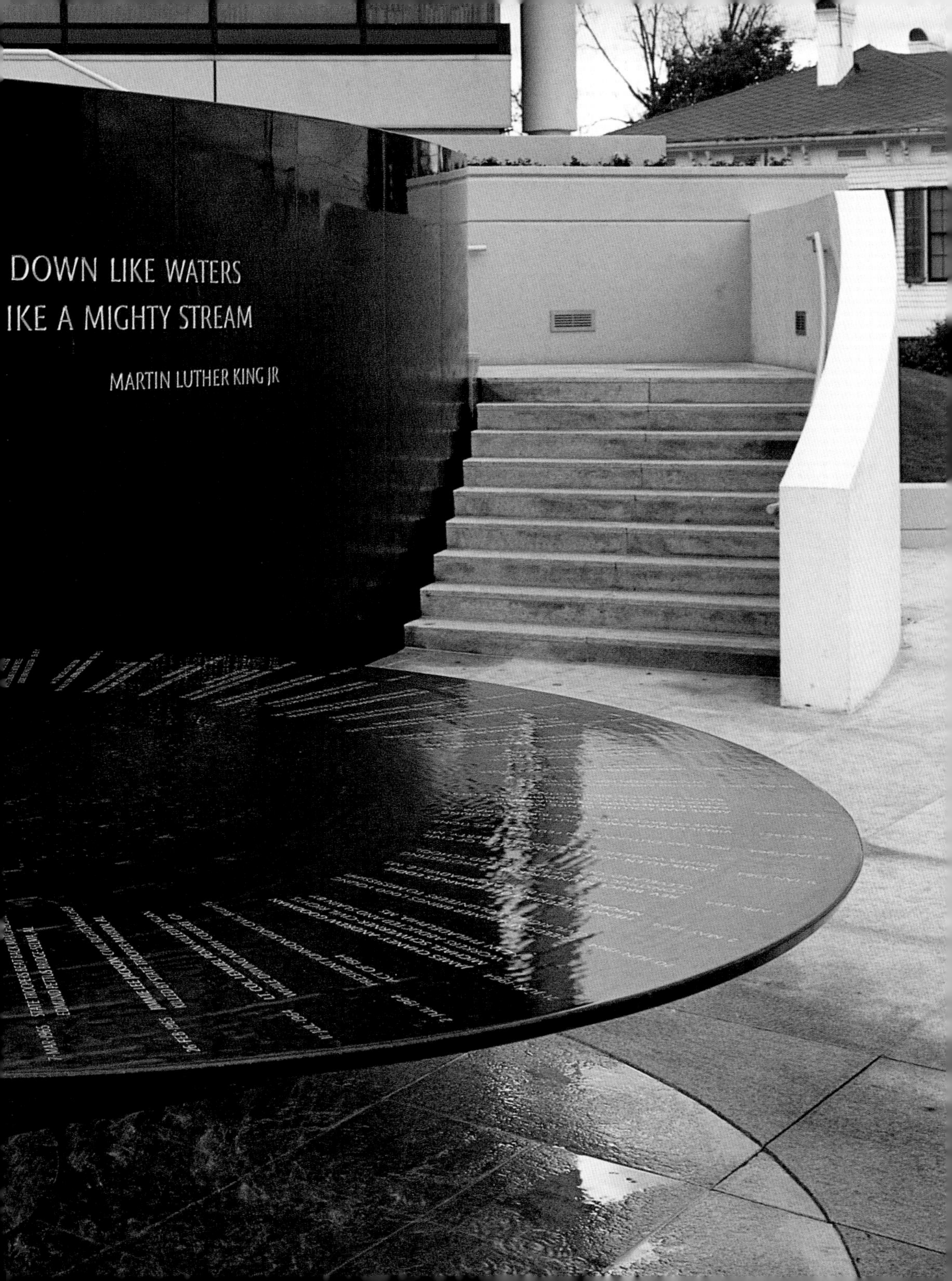
DOWN LIKE WATERS
IKE A MIGHTY STREAM
MARTIN LUTHER KING JR

Maya collaborated with the SPLC and historians on the text. "I wanted it to tell the history without becoming too emotional or sensational," she said. Maya decided to simply list key dates of the civil rights movement along the outer edge of the sculpture, which is 12 feet (3.7 metres) in diameter. Intertwined with those events are the names of forty people who were killed. Maya said, "I was trying to illustrate the cause-and-effect relationship."

A walk around the sculpture shows how the act of a single person, or a death, led to a new and better law. The timeline begins with May 17, 1954, when after reviewing the case *Brown v. Board of Education*, the U.S. Supreme Court outlawed segregation in schools. And it ends with April 4, 1968, the day Dr. King was assassinated. Maya purposely left a space after the inscription for 1968 to show that this timeline is not closed. She realized that the civil rights movement didn't have a definite beginning or end. The struggle for racial equality continues.

As with the Vietnam Veterans Memorial, she chose to use black granite for the memorial. But this time she left the stone unpolished. It becomes shiny and reflective only when it is covered with water. Using water presented technical problems, such as controlling the flow of water, that Maya worked with a special team of fabricators to solve. During the entire process Maya was on the job wearing her customary turtleneck sweater, black pants, and boots. More grown-up now, she had cut her knee-length hair and wore it pulled back into a short ponytail.

Dedication of the memorial took place on November 5, 1989. More than six thousand people attended and sang "We Shall Overcome," an anthem of the civil rights movement symbolizing unity and deter-mination. Among those gathered were well-known civil rights veterans Rosa Parks and Julian Bond, as well as rel-atives of the victims whose names were inscribed on the timeline. Carolyn Goodman, mother of Andrew Goodman, killed on June 21, 1964, in Philadelphia, Mississippi, was there, and so was Mamie Till Mobley, mother of Emmett Till, a fourteen-year-old who was murdered on August 28, 1955, in Money, Mississippi.

As people gathered around the timeline table and touched the names carved into the stone, they created

ripples. Maya realized that the tears they shed fell onto the table and became a part of it. This was exactly what she had intended. She said,

> "I wanted people to be able to feel like they really were a part of making this piece come alive."

- Of the forty victims listed on the Civil Rights Memorial, none of their murderers were convicted until 1994 because of racism in the federal courts.

Earth

CHAPTER FOUR: Wave Field

As children, Maya and her brother played on the hills behind their house. "A strong respect and love for the land exists throughout my work," says Maya. "I grew up surrounded by woods. I loved that landscape. The privacy." There were three ridges separated by streams and Maya called the middle one the lizard's back. "It started up from the creek bed, like a tail," she recalled. "It grew into a long winding ridge, and ended in what to us looked like the head of a lizard."

That image stayed with her and profoundly influenced her outdoor artwork *Wave Field*. "When I go out of doors," said Maya, "I'm literally my father's daughter. My dad was a ceramicist. I'm sculpting the earth."

The *Wave Field* project began in 1993 when Maya was asked to create a sculpture for the University of Michigan's

Children run through *Storm King Wavefield* at Storm King Art Center in Mountainville, New York.

new aerospace engineering building. It was dedicated to the memory of F. X. Bagnoud, a Michigan graduate who had died flying helicopter rescue missions in Africa.

Maya was eager to pursue her interest in earthwork, and so she accepted the commission. She visited the site and thought about what the building was going to be used for. She wanted her earth sculpture to connect with the classes, such as the mechanics of flight, that would be taught inside the building. Once again she began with research. She wrote,

> " Each project allows me to learn about a new subject. "

She talked to professors in the department and read about the way air moves around an object. As she read about aerodynamics, she became intrigued by images depicting turbulence: irregular winds that affect airplanes and give passengers a bumpy ride. One day she came across a photograph that grabbed her attention. It showed a Stokes wave, an example of repetitive water waves. "The image was the one I knew I had been looking for," she wrote.

Maya sketching a design for *Eleven Minute Line*, an earth artwork in Sweden that was inspired by the Serpent Mound in Ohio where she grew up.

Maya began making three-dimensional models of the wave in clay and sand. Then she was ready to move on to the actual sculpture. But it was difficult for her to grasp how one water wave begins and another one ends. Maya said, "I spent hours looking at the ocean, trying to see a beginning or an end, but of course there isn't one." Her goal was to make the forms appear natural.

Collaborating with landscape architects, she concocted a sandy soil mix that would drain well and hold its shape during Michigan's rain and snow. Maya didn't want puddles settling at the bottom of her waves. And then they began to create earthen walls that stood 3 to 6 feet (0.9 to 1.8 metres) high.

In the final weeks of grading, or shaping the angle of the walls, Maya worked with the landscape contractors. "I physically hand-raked and detailed each wave form," she wrote. In the fall of 1994, grass was planted on the waves, but in order to allow time for it to grow, it would be a year before anyone could visit it.

At last Maya invited students to walk through *Wave Field* and become part of the sculpture. "Its scale is such that you can sit in a wave, curl up, and read a book if you

Maya outdoors drawing at the site of *Storm King Wavefield.*

like," she told them. Kids love to climb over the waves and play games. Families have picnics. And viewed from ground level or classrooms above, the work appears to change its shape as the sunlight casts different shadows throughout the day.

Maya continued to be fascinated by land sculpture. In 2005 she designed *Flutter* for the Federal Courthouse in Miami, Florida. *Flutter*, the second in her series of earth waves, is based on sand patterns *underneath* the ocean waves.

The third and largest work in the series is *Storm King Wavefield*, located in the Storm King Art Center, a vast sculpture park in Mountainville, New York.

After being commissioned to design an earth sculpture there, Maya visited the park. She saw an eleven-acre gravel pit. The gravel had been used in creating the New York State Thruway and other projects in the park, and grass was starting to grow on the surrounding hillside. Maya responded immediately. She liked the idea that the project would involve environmental work as she restored the pit.

Maya made sketches and calculations. Then construction began on July 15, 2007. She teamed up with landscape

A professor and students relax in the waves of *Wave Field*, University of Michigan.

architects and used gravel from the pit as well as more rock and topsoil to construct rolling rows of waves. Maya drove up from New York City every week to check on the piece's progress and to shape it exactly as she wanted it.

Storm King Wavefield consists of seven rows of grassy waves. The waves have the same scale as an actual set of waves, some as high as 15 feet (4.5 metres), more than twice the height of an adult. Maya helped with almost every aspect of the work except for operating the bulldozer. The final step was planting warm-weather grasses on the four and a half acres of waves.

In July 2008 the piece was finished and open to the public. Visitors can behold *Storm King Wavefield* from a tram ride on the road, or they can climb uphill along a path to capture incredible views. "Amazing!" is a comment often heard at first sighting, for the linked curves really look like cresting ocean waves. Maya said that walking through the earthwork gives a person an experience similar to being at sea. "It is initially disconcerting," wrote an art critic who felt a little seasick as he strolled along *Storm King Wavefield* even though he was on land.

● Maya directing the earthmover during construction of *Storm King Wavefield*.

The work changes dramatically through the seasons. In the spring and summer patches of buttercups and clover bloom alongside the green mounds, adding color. And in winter the waves turn white as they are covered with snow. Maya said,

> " What I'm trying to do is allow you to pay attention to beautiful forms in nature. "

Storm King Wavefield echos the rolling hills that surround it and changes with the seasons.

Glass

In 1998 Maya was asked to design a library. But this was not going to be any ordinary library. It was to be used as a reading room and conference center for the Children's Defense Fund (CDF). The CDF is a nonprofit organization dedicated to helping American children, especially those living in poverty.

In 1994 the CDF purchased the Haley Farm in Clinton, Tennessee, to use as a retreat for leadership training. The large farm had belonged to Alex Haley, an African American writer whose award-winning novel *Roots* had been made into one of the most popular television series of all time. *Roots* traced the history of Haley's family, going back to one of his ancestors, an African captured, enslaved, and brought to Virginia.

The Langston Hughes Library features books by African American authors and books about the black experience for readers of all ages.

The CDF wanted to have a library that would feature works by and about African Americans, to inspire young leaders.

When Maya visited the Haley Farm, to her delight she found an old barn that had been built in the 1860s. It was a typical Tennessee cantilevered barn, with the upper level extending beyond the vertical supports. The barn perched on top of two corncribs made of rough logs. The cribs were for storing dried corn that was used as winterfeed for animals. Maya loved the building. She said,

> "**I'd never seen a shape like that before and wanted to save it.**"

She came up with the concept of an elevated reading room. "The idea was to maintain the integrity and character of the old barn yet introduce a new inner layer."

Maya kept the silvery outside of the barn, but she took apart the inside. Working with Knoxville architect Margaret Butler, Maya dismantled beams and rebuilt the

● The Langston Hughes Library's reading room honors writer and civil rights activist Dr. Maya Angelou, and Dr. John Hope Franklin, a leading scholar of black history.

structure. She "slipped in" a steel foundation underneath for support and created an entirely new interior. For the cozy yet airy reading room, she used recycled, environmentally friendly materials, such as soybean husks for the tabletops. To bring the outside in, she designed a large picture window in front of the reading area with views of the pond and trees. Rows of skylights provide even more natural light. Maya said she wanted people in the library to "always feel connected to the land."

Below, she wrapped the cribs in an inner layer of translucent glass. Rays of light shine between the logs. She said, "As you walk inside, you see the shadow of the exterior timbers." One crib contains a bookstore, and the other has a stairway and elevator to the upper level. In the space between the cribs Maya designed a garden with a stone fountain that marks the entrance to the library.

The project was completed in 1999. An art critic for the *Seattle Post-Intelligencer* wrote that Maya had transformed the barn into a "marvel of colored light and air." Margaret Butler said it "glows like a Chinese lantern."

The Langston Hughes Library shines brightly and illuminates the night.

The library was named for Langston Hughes, an African American poet who celebrated the lives of ordinary black people. In his poem "My People" he wrote,

The night is beautiful,
So the faces of my people.

His complete works are in the library's collection along with thousands of books for children and adults on subjects ranging from African American history and the civil rights movement to fine arts and literature from many writers and cultures.

The reading room was dedicated to poet and novelist Dr. Maya Angelou and historian Dr. John Hope Franklin. They both attended the dedication ceremony on March 19, 1999, along with First Lady Hillary Rodham Clinton. Of course, Maya Lin and her family were there, too. By this time Maya was married to Daniel Wolf, a photography dealer and collector of pre-Columbian furniture and crystals. Like Maya, he is passionate about art as well as the outdoors. Their daughter, India, had been born in 1998, a few months before Maya began the library project.

● Dedication ceremony of the Langston Hughes Library in 1999. From left to right:
Frank Diggs, mayor of Clinton, Tennessee; Marian Wright Edelman, founder of
CDF; Hillary Rodham Clinton, First Lady and former CDF board chair; Len Riggio,
CDF board member; and Maya Lin.

A few months after she completed the project, Maya gave birth to another daughter, Rachel.

While raising her children, Maya continued to work in her studio designing private houses and public parks and making small sculptures. She started an environmental project in the Pacific Northwest and wrote an autobiography, titled *Boundaries*. "I do a lot of projects at once," she says. But after the terrorist attacks on September 11, 2001, everything changed. "My love of creating disappeared," she said. "I think a lot of artists felt similarly lost."

Then the CDF asked her to design another project—an interfaith chapel on Haley Farm. They wanted to give people a place to find comfort and peace. Maya was moved and accepted the commission. She said, "Working on a spiritually based project that focused on helping others was the only thing that could get me to start making things again."

A drawing of a small boat on a stormy sea by a seven-year-old girl that was featured in the CDF logo sparked an idea. The boat reminded Maya of Noah's ark, a symbol of shelter and protection. She envisioned a simple wooden structure that would be shaped like an ark. Maya said that

DEAR LORD
BE GOOD TO ME
THE SEA IS SO
WIDE AND
MY BOAT IS
SO SMALL

Children's Defense Fund

The CDF logo contains a prayer that founder Marian Wright Edelman first saw on a desktop ship in the office of Robert F. Kennedy, the U.S. attorney general from 1961 to 1964 and an advocate for the civil rights movement.

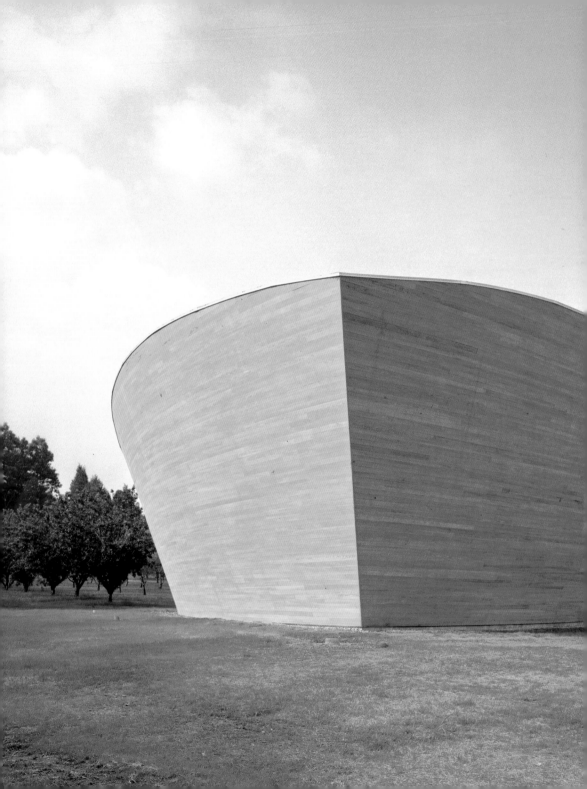

her design expressed the purpose of the CDF, "to carry the nation's family of children to safe harbor."

The chapel is situated near a pond across from the library. For the outside of the building she used locally grown cypress. Inside, the ceiling has curved beams that arch overhead like embracing arms. There are no windows, but natural light pours in through skylights. Maya said,

> "My goal was to quietly raise people's hope and elevate their spirits through beautiful surroundings."

● The Riggio-Lynch Chapel, which resembles a huge ark, seats 250 people.

Celadon

CHAPTER SIX: The Museum of
Chinese in America

Growing up, Maya never knew much about her parents'
background. Then, on her twenty-first birthday, she and
her family attended a party at the Chinese embassy in
Washington, D.C. Maya's father spoke with the Chinese
ambassador for a long time. Afterward Maya said, "What
were you talking about?" And her father began telling her
about his family's history.

It turned out that Maya's grandfather had been a well-
known scholar. And her aunt had been an architect and
architectural historian in Beijing. She had come to the
United States to study architecture at the University of
Pennsylvania, but she was not admitted because she was
a woman. However, within a year she wound up on the
faculty. The story fascinated Maya. "All the female Lins

Visitors to the museum study a timeline tracing 160 years
of Chinese American history.

are very strong, very independent," her father said. "All very talented and very determined."

Maya's mother also had a remarkable history. She had been smuggled out of Shanghai as a teenager, and friends in America helped her get a scholarship to Smith College. A poet and a teacher, she completed her Ph.D. at the University of Washington when Maya and her brother, Tan, were young children. "She worked on her books and on her teaching career and took care of us," said Maya. The accomplishments of her mother and aunt were inspiring.

In 1986, when Maya was twenty-seven and doing her graduate work at Yale, her mother took her and Tan to China to meet relatives for the first time. Maya's father stayed home because he was too ill to travel. But on the trip they visited the place in Fujian Province where he had lived as a boy. Maya was amazed that, unlike traditional Chinese houses, her grandfather's house was built in a Japanese style. "It was a house overlooking the river, with two or three courtyards," she said. "Spaces flowed through sliding screens . . . It was just magical. I was blown away. I had an affinity to this place."

As a result of this trip, Maya became more aware of her heritage and wanted to learn more about the Chinese American experience. So, in 2004, when the Museum of Chinese in America (MOCA) asked her to lead a design team to expand the museum, she agreed. MOCA had been located in cramped quarters on the second floor of an old school building in lower Manhattan. Maya found a bigger place, a former machine repair shop on the edge of Chinatown. "There was a courtyard there, but they had hidden it away," she said. "We went poking around the basement, which was pretty rank." The space reminded her of her grandfather's house in Fujian Province built around a courtyard. "It's not that I'm literally trying to re-create that in the museum," said Maya.

"Going down those stairs is like seeing where you come from."

Maya designed the exhibition spaces around the courtyard. She left the brick walls bare but added a large skylight overhead. Films about Chinese Americans are projected

on windows facing the courtyard. Photographs and other artifacts are presented throughout the museum. Maya's husband contributed vintage photos, some from his own collection. Also on display are newspapers published in the late nineteenth century with articles about discrimination and the passage of the Chinese Exclusion Act, in 1882, which prevented Chinese laborers from coming to the United States because of their nationality.

One area is devoted to Angel Island in San Francisco, a place where Chinese immigrants were held and questioned before being allowed to enter the United States. Many wrote poems on the wooden walls of the detention center expressing their misery, and their words are reproduced in the museum.

It's been seven weeks since my imprisonment
On this island—and still I do not know when I can land.

There is a re-creation of a successful Chinatown grocery store from nineteenth-century New York City. Glass-fronted cabinets hold the actual tea, spices, and canned

Videos telling personal stories of Chinese Americans are projected on the brick walls of the museum's interior courtyard.

goods that were sold in the store. There are also galleries showing American stereotypes of Chinese culture: chewable Chinese checkers called "Fu Man Chews," a movie poster for *Charlie Chan at the Opera*, and a glowing neon sign saying "Chop Suey." Farther on an exhibit tells about "Red China" and the communist scare in the United States in the 1950s.

Although the color red is important in Chinese tradition, Maya remembered the dresses her mother made her wear as a child and detested it. So for the museum's graphics Maya used celadon green, a soft shade that was the color of a type of glaze used on ancient Chinese ceramics. Green had another meaning for her as well. "The building is completely green," she said, "in the sense that it uses recycled materials, sustainably harvested woods." Despite Maya's objection, the curators still featured red in the museum. For instance, there's a timeline of major events in the history of the Chinese in America that is printed on red blocks.

In the lobby Maya designed a Journey Wall made of bronze tiles. The tiles are engraved with the names of

● The museum includes a re-creation of a general store that was located in New York City's Chinatown in the late nineteenth century.

Chinese families, their place of origin, and their home in America. Maya donated a tile in honor of her parents. It reads: Julia Ming-hui Lin and Henry Huan Lin, Shanghai and Fuchow, Athens, Ohio. A plaque at the end of the permanent exhibition states Maya's intention. It says,

> **"I think of my work as creating a private conversation with each person, no matter how public each work is and no matter how many people are present."**

● The museum helps bring the stories of Chinese immigrants alive through multimedia exhibits like "With a Single Step." Portraits of Chinese immigrants who came to America in the early twentieth century dangle from the ceiling.

Dunes and Driftwood

CHAPTER SEVEN: The Confluence Project

In 2000 a group in Washington State called the Confluence Project wanted to commemorate the bicentennial of Lewis and Clark's expedition. The expedition party had spent eighteen days in Washington in 1805 on their journey to reach the Pacific Ocean. The group from the Confluence Project called Maya and asked her to design a memorial.

"Absolutely not," she said once again.

Washington's governor, Gary Locke, was a friend of Maya's. He, too, was of Chinese descent and a graduate of Yale. He called Maya and said, "Would you just meet with the Confluence people?"

"I'm not in the monument business," she replied.

Then to her surprise, tribal elders of the Nez Perce, Umatilla, and Chinook, who were part of the Confluence

A child and her grandmother admire Baker Bay from the viewing platform at Cape Disappointment.

Project, came to her studio in New York City. They said, "Lewis and Clark did not come into an uninhabited land. They didn't discover this country [the Pacific Northwest]. We were here. We think you could share and understand and delve deeper." They told Maya about the ecological changes over the years. While gathering information about plants and animals, Lewis and Clark had brought illness and destruction. As the elders talked about the river and the salmon, she grew interested.

But Maya had just launched her project *What Is Missing?* about the extinction of species. She told the elders that if she accepted their project, she wouldn't be able to get to it for another five years.

They agreed to wait.

It took Maya three years to figure out how she would approach the project. In the meantime, she was working on many other things: designing furniture, making *Timetable* for Stanford University, and constructing the Riggio-Lynch Chapel. And, of course, she was raising her children.

Finally, Maya began to really focus on Confluence. Her goal was not celebration as much as understanding. She wanted to encourage people to look at the land as it is today and as it was in the past, from different points of view. She planned six locations along the Columbia River for the project. "Each one tells you what went on at that place," she explained. "We started with Cape Disappointment, where Lewis and Clark ended . . . where the river meets the sea." For Maya this was like "holding up a mirror to reflect back upon Lewis and Clark's journey."

Cape Disappointment State Park is located at the mouth of the Columbia River. Working with park planners and landscape designers, Maya replaced parking lots with natural dunes and native grasses. Her objective was to remind people of what had been lost and what could be saved. She said,

> "A lot of my work is not very glorious. If I succeed, you may never know I was here."

Maya installed a new fish-cleaning table near the boat launch. She selected a block of local basalt rock for the table. It has a sink carved into it on one end and is

The fish-cleaning table at Cape Disappointment.

engraved with a Chinook creation myth about how the Chinook tribe came to be.

The story tells of an old man who met a giantess. The man caught a little whale and the giantess told him to split it down the back. But the man cut the whale the wrong way. The whale changed into a thunderbird that flew to the top of a mountain near the Columbia River and laid a nest of eggs. And from the eggs came the first members of mankind.

Maya said of the story, "It's also a reminder that Chinook fishermen were catching salmon here thousands of years before white men came." The words of the myth etched in the rock were intended to grip the fish when they're being cleaned. Chinook chief Cliff Snider says the salmon slip off the polished table, but nonetheless he is appreciative of Maya's respectful treatment of his people's history.

Maya had first thought that the Native Americans and Lewis and Clark had followed the same path to the ocean. But she realized there were two different walkways. Lewis and Clark had made a "beeline to the ocean." So she designed a boardwalk leading to a viewing platform

● Maya Lin and Horace Axtell, a Nez Perce tribal elder, celebrate the dedication at Chief Timothy Park, a Confluence Project site in the Nez Perce homeland in Washington State.

WE CALL UPON THE EARTH OUR PLANET HOME,
WITH ITS BEAUTIFUL DEPTHS AND SOARING HEIGHTS,
ITS VITALITY AND ABUNDANCE OF LIFE,
AND TOGETHER WE ASK THAT IT

TEACH US, AND SHOW US THE WAY.

at the beach that is inscribed with excerpts from Clark's journal, using his original spelling.

"Saw several rattle snakes."
"Saw several Canoes."
"Ocian in view! O! the joy."

Another trail follows the original water's edge and leads to a totem circle made of cedar driftwood. This is the Chinook homeland. On November 18, 2005, the very date that Lewis and Clark had arrived at the spot two hundred years earlier, the Chinook blessed the site. The blessing opens, "We call upon the earth, our planet home, with its beautiful depths and soaring heights, its vitality and abundance of life, and together we ask that it Teach us and show us the way."

Maya was so moved by the beauty of the dedication that she asked for permission to include it in the project. It is now engraved on the Blessing Trail.

The entire Chinook blessing consists of eight sections that are engraved along the Blessing Trail.

Wood

CHAPTER EIGHT: The Box House

When people ask Maya to design a house for them, her answer is usually no. "I can't take on too many projects," she says. But in 2006 she accepted a commission to design a mountain retreat in Telluride, Colorado, for Charles Price and his wife. The Price family had a history of engaging great American architects. In 1952 Charles Price's grand-father, Harold Price, had commissioned Frank Lloyd Wright, one of the most innovative architects of the twentieth century, to design an office building for him in Bartlesville, Oklahoma. So Charles followed tradition when he asked Maya to develop the project in Colorado.

"I love the Price house," says Maya. "It's my Box House." The house consists of two rectangular wooden boxes connected by outdoor decks. Set at the edge of an aspen forest in the Rocky Mountains, floor-to-ceiling glass

The Box House has slatted shutters to prevent birds from flying into the large windows.

windows bring the outside in. Each window frames a particular view selected by Maya. Mrs. Price said, "We asked Maya to design the house because it is a pretty spot and we did not want to destroy it." A double-trunked aspen tree grows right through openings in the middle of the decks. "I love to give people outdoor rooms," Maya explains.

Inside, the house has no standard walls. Hidden panels and doors slide open to create privacy for bedrooms and bathrooms. Or they disappear to allow one room to flow into the next. "The design [of the Box House] has a secretive element. I wanted to create a space that could change," said Maya.

"I think of how people live in and move through the space."

Maya was inspired by Asian toy puzzle boxes, which have hidden compartments and sliding parts. Sliding the parts in the correct order opens the toy box and reveals a good-luck charm inside.

"The Box House may be deceptively simple," said Maya. "It's also quite playful."

● A view of the Box House showing an aspen tree growing through the decks that connect the larger section to the smaller box, which has a guest room and garage.

Box House with the Colorado Rocky Mountains in the distance.

Memories

CHAPTER NINE: What Is Missing?

Every twenty minutes a living plant or animal species disappears because of humans. Maya asked herself,

"What can I do as an artist?"

And she came up with the idea for a multimedia project called *What Is Missing?* She says, "I want to wake people up to species loss and habitat loss. And suggest things we can all do to help. How can we protect and restore nature? Art can get people to pay closer attention."

Maya set up her own nonprofit foundation in 2003 to fund the memorial. Then over the next five years she and her assistants and many volunteers gathered more than six hundred testimonies from people on every continent

The author and a child watching a video in the *Listening Cone* at the California Academy of Sciences in San Francisco.

and planned a website that features charts, maps, and educational videos.

In 2009 Maya installed the first part of the project at the California Academy of Sciences, in San Francisco. It's a huge sculpture called the *Listening Cone*. Made of bronze and redwood, it's shaped like a gigantic megaphone. Children and adults can crawl inside and curl up to watch videos of endangered and extinct species and hear their sounds.

Javan rhinoceros. Jaguar. Lion. Bat. Prairie chicken. Humpback whale.

Some people like sitting in it too long, and that can be a problem when other visitors are waiting for a turn.

In addition to the permanent *Listening Cone*, the memorial includes traveling exhibits and an interactive website. People of all ages are invited to go online and share their memories, or stories they've heard from parents and grandparents, about once-common creatures and plants that are disappearing. One man wrote that when he was a boy in Pittsburgh, Pennsylvania, "all it took was a jar and five minutes in anybody's backyard

The *Listening Cone* at the California Academy of Sciences in San Francisco features a selection of seventy-five videos with texts linking threatened and endangered species to their habitats.

to capture dozens of fireflies, to be enjoyed and set free."
Now he can't remember the last time he saw a dozen fireflies in an entire evening.

One video in the exhibit is called "Unchopping a Tree."
The movie shows a redwood tree being chopped down
until it is just a stump. Then, the film goes backward and
at the end of the movie the redwood magically appears
whole again. The film urges people not to chop down
trees—or if they do, to plant new ones in their place. Maya
says, "Together we can save two birds with one tree."

Maya Lin received a National Medal of the Arts. This is
the nation's highest honor for artistic excellence. Maya
was recognized for "her profound work as an architect,
artist, and environmentalist." And in 2016, she received the
Medal of Freedom from President Barack Obama as well.

But Maya is not content to rest on her achievements.
She continues to push the boundaries of what a memorial
can be. The newest part of *What Is Missing?* is a sculpture
called *Sound Ring*. It was installed in 2014 at the Cornell
Lab of Ornithology, in Ithaca, New York. Maya developed it
with scientists at the lab. The ring, 9 feet (2.7 metres) high,

In 2010 Maya received the 2009 National Medal of Arts from President
Barack Obama, who said, "The arts and humanities appeal to a certain
yearning that's shared by all of us."

has hidden speakers that play the sounds of threatened species: toots of lemurs, wails of loons, and nighthawks booming "who-hoo." There is even an underwater recording of Weddell seals in Antarctica.

At the unveiling Maya said, "We can't do anything about what has already been lost, but can we learn enough from the past to rethink a different and better future?"

The memorial is a work in progress that presents an ecological history of the planet. So far, forty scientists and conservationists around the world are participating. The project will end with Greenprint for the Future, a series of e-books and booklets that will offer people ways to protect the planet, such as changing their diets—for instance, eating less meat to save natural resources, growing native plants instead of lawns to reduce the need for water, and using solar power to reduce the use of fossil fuels. "There's a lot we can do," she said. "We could all make a difference."

Although Maya continues to juggle many exciting art and architecture projects in her studio, as well as take care of her teenage daughters at home, she dedicates much of her time to the *What Is Missing?* project.

"It's my last memorial. It will probably take my lifetime and beyond . . . If you give nature a chance, the world can heal."

ACKNOWLEDGMENTS

Most of all I want to thank Maya Lin for her generous and gracious cooperation. Thanks also to her studio manager, James Ewart, for his enormous help. At the Pace Gallery I am indebted to Lindsay McGuire and Heather Monahan. And a special thank you to David R. Collens, director and curator of Storm King Art Center. At Chronicle I want to express gratitude to my editor, Victoria Rock, for passionately pursuing this book. I also thank her assistant, Taylor Norman, and the talented designer Kayla Ferriera.

Thanks to Theresa Venable and Patti Hassler at the Langston Hughes Library, Chun Yee Yip O'Neill and Sophie Lo at the Museum of Chinese in America, and Steve Wood, interpretive specialist at the Cape Disappointment State Park.

My dear friend and agent, George Nicholson, gave me invaluable advice and encouragement, and I will always be grateful. I also want to express gratitude to his assistant, Caitlin MacDonald, and to his colleague Erica Silverman, who stepped in to help me.

Finally a big bouquet of thanks to my writer friends at Lunch Bunch, my son Andrew, and my husband, Michael, for their cheering support.

BIBLIOGRAPHY

Books

Andrews, Richard. *Maya Lin: Storm King Wavefield*. Mountainville, New York: Storm King Art Center, 2009.

Bunting, Eve. *The Wall*. New York: Clarion Books, 1990.

Hughes, Langston. *The Collected Poems*. Arnold Rampersad, Editor. New York: Knopf, 1994.

Lashnits, Tom. *Maya Lin*. New York: Chelsea House, 2007.

Lin, Maya. *Boundaries*. New York: Simon & Schuster, 2000.

—. *Here and There*. New York: Pace Gallery, 2013.

Malone, Mary. *Maya Lin: Architect and Artist*. Springfield, NJ: Enslow Books, 1995.

Booklet

What Is Missing? New York: What Is Missing? Foundation, 2014.

Articles

Academy of Achievement. "Maya Lin: Artist and Architect." June 16, 2000. http://www.achievement.org/autodoc/printmember/lin0int-1.

Amelar, Sarah. "Inspired by Asian Puzzle Toys, Maya Lin Rafts the Kinetic Box House, Opening It Quietly to High Peaks in the Colorado Rockies." *Architectural Record*, April 2006.

Bernstein, Fred. "Maya Lin: A Portrait of the Memorial Designer as Architect and Artist." http://www.fredbernstein.com/articles/display.asp?id=47.

Brown, Patricia Leigh. "At Home With: Maya Lin; Making History On a Human Scale." *The New York Times*, May 21, 1998.

Castro, Jan Garden. "One Who Sees Space: A Conversation with Maya Lin." September 2002. http://www.sculpture.org/documents/scmago2/sept02/lin/lin.shtml.

Cohen, Margot. "The Collector: Maya Lin." *The Wall Street Journal*, March 29, 2010. http://online.wsj.com/articles/SB126708083973951315.

Cook, Richard. "Price's Wright." *Wallpaper*, June/July 2008.

Cotter, Holland. "Where the Ocean Meets the Mountains." *New York Times*, May 7, 2009.

Covington, Elizabeth. "Box House on the Mesa." *Shelter, Telluride's Home & Living Magazine*, summer 2007.

Dameron, Amanda. Q & A with Architectural Designer & Artists Maya Lin, *Dwell*, April 2013.

Davidson, Justin. "Maya Lin's Big Dig." *New York Magazine*, August 24, 2009.

Fitzpatrick, John. "The Sound Ring." Living on Earth, week of August 29, 2014. Transcript: http://www.loe.org/shows/segments/html?programID=14-P13-00035&segmentID=6.

Gopnik, Adam. "Stones and Bones: Visiting the 9/11 Memorial and Museum." *New Yorker*, July 7 & 14, 2014.

Guilbert, Juliette. "Reversing Course." *Metropolis Magazine*, November 2008.

Hackett, Regina. "Maya Lin's Courage: The Artist Who Created the Vietnam Veterans Memorial Emerges from the Shadows with a Book and a More Outspoken Profile." *Seattle Post-Intelligencer*, October 19, 2000.

Kino, Carol. "Maya Lin's New Memorial Is a City." *New York Times*, April 28, 2013.

Kreyling, Christine. "Lin Finds New Use for Old Barn at Langston Hughes Library." *Architectural Record*, May 2000.

Leonard, Pat. "Maya Lin's 'Sound Ring' unveiled at Lab of Ornithology." *Cornell Chronicle*, June 3, 2014.

Menand, Louis. "The Reluctant Memorialist." *The New Yorker*, July 8, 2002.

Menand, Louis. "Maya Lin and the Vietnam Veterans Memorial." *The History Reader*, March 27, 2012.

Moyers, Bill. Interview with Maya Lin. "Becoming American." Public Affairs Television, 2003. http://www.pbs.org/becomingamerican/ap_pjourneys_transcript5.html.

Parfit, Michael. "35 Who Made a Difference: Maya Lin." *Smithsonian Magazine*, November 2005.

Reed, Amanda. "What Is Missing?: Maya Lin's Memorial on the Sixth Extinction." *World-changing Archives,* October 12, 2010. http://www.worldchanging.com/archives/011645.html.

Rothstein, Edward. "Reopened Museum Tells Chinese-American Stories." *New York Times*, September 21, 2009.

Sarasohn, David. "A Confluence of the Past, the Present and a River." February 18, 2013. http://www.oregonlive.com/news/oregonian/david_sarasohn/index.ssf/2013/02/david.html.

Spica, Heather Joyner. "Maya Lin launches good month for Design Lab." *Metro Pulse Online*, August 5, 2004, vol.14, no.32.

Thomas, Mary. "Maya Lin invites and challenges visitors to her website to help improve Earth's well-being." *Pittsburgh Post-Gazette*, April 18, 2012.

Vaadia, Sara. "An Evening with Maya Lin." *Fearless and Loathing: Oberlin's Independent Student Website,* April 12, 2013. http://www.fearlessandloathing.com/2013/04/an-evening-with-maya-lin.

Wills, Denise Kersten. "The Vietnam Memorial's History." *Washingtonian*, November 1, 2007.

Videos

Maya Lin: A Strong Clear Vision. Written and directed by Freida Lee Mock, produced by Freida Lee Mock, Terry Sanders. 1994. American Film Foundation Production, New Video Group, Inc., 2003. Marketed and distributed by New Video. DVD.

Radio broadcast

OPB radio programs, November 11, 2010, 9 A.M., updated September 10, 2013, 9:43 P.M.

Interviews

Author with Maya Lin, June 17, 2014.

SOURCE NOTES

p. IV— "You need . . . *and* memorials." Author interview with Maya Lin, June 17, 2014.

p. V— "I was making . . . still am." Author interview with Maya Lin, June 17, 2014.

Chapter One

p. 1— "So I made . . . my own world." Academy of Achievement, "Maya Lin: Artist and Architect." June 16, 2000.

p. 1— "precious stone." J. G. Castro, "One Who Sees Space." September 2002.

p. 1— "My father . . . a poet." M. Lin, *Boundaries*, p. 5:04.

p. 2— "He worked . . . effortlessly." *Boundaries*, p. 7:03.

p. 2— "My mother . . . color red!" M. Cohen, "The Collector: Maya Lin." March 29, 2010.

p. 2— "For them . . . the past." *Boundaries*, p. 5:04.

p. 2— "When I . . . be censored." Academy of Achievement, "Maya Lin: Artist and Architect." June 16, 2000.

p. 4— "two heritages . . . was white . . . American as possible." Academy of Achievement, "Maya Lin: Artist and Architect." June 16, 2000.

p. 4— "I studied . . . Class A nerd . . . have any friends." Academy of Achievement, "Maya Lin: Artist and Architect." June 16, 2000.

p. 4–5— "One time . . . didn't hear anything." Academy of Achievement, "Maya Lin: Artist and Architect." June 16, 2000.

p. 5— "I was the . . . to the football games." Academy of Achievement, "Maya Lin: Artist and Architect." June 16, 2000.

Chapter Two

p. 7— "the dumbest." Academy of Achievement, "Maya Lin: Artist and Architect." June 16, 2000.

p. 7— "For the . . . fit in." L. Menand, "The Reluctant Memorialist." July 8, 2002.

p. 7— "It was . . . art and science." Academy of Achievement, "Maya Lin: Artist and Architect." June 16, 2000.

p. 8– "news-conscious." B. Moyers interview, "Becoming American." 2003.

p. 8— "What exactly . . . should it do?" *Boundaries*, p. 4:08.

p. 8— "I try . . . a 'what.'" B. Moyers Interview, "Becoming American." 2003.

p. 8— "Many of . . . those who died." *Boundaries*, p. 4:09.

p. 10— "I had . . . marble walls." *Boundaries*, p. 4:09.

p. 10— "respond and remember." *Boundaries*, p. 4:10.

p. 10— "At the . . . into the earth." *Boundaries*, p. 4:10.

p. 12— "I wanted . . . too little." *Boundaries*, p. 4:11.

p. 12— "I think . . . my hands." *Boundaries*, p. 3:09.

p. 12— "My brother . . . entire childhoods." A. Dameron, Q & A with Maya Lin. April 2013.

p. 12— "eccentric." *Boundaries*, p. 7:03.

p. 15— "It took . . . the memorial." *Boundaries*, 4:11.

p. 15— "It never . . . an exercise." *Boundaries*, p. 4:12.

p. 16— "I think . . . mine did." *Boundaries*, p. 4:12.

p. 16— "I often . . . been selected?" *Boundaries*, p. 4:15.

p. 16— "I immediately . . . to completion." *Boundaries*, p. 4:13.

p. 18— "I fought . . . listing." *Boundaries*, p. 4:13.

p. 18— "too *feminine*." *Boundaries*, p. 4:14.

p. 18— "shame and dishonor." *Boundaries*, p. 4:15.

p. 18— "a dark . . . the dead." *Boundaries*, p. 4:14.

p. 18— "black scar." T. Lashnits, *Maya Lin*, p. 33.

p. 19— "inappropriate." *Boundaries*, p. 4:16.

p. 19— "veterans would . . . and uplifting." *Boundaries*, p. 4:16.

p. 19— "violate . . . private contemplative space." *Boundaries*, p. 4:17.

p. 19— "I was . . . anyone else." *Boundaries*, p. 5:06.

p. 19–20— "I wanted . . . forget it." R. Hackett, "Maya Lin's Courage." October 19, 2000.

p. 20— "It was . . . totally public." *Boundaries*, p. 4:16.

p. 20— "The first time I visited the memorial . . . designed it." *Boundaries*, p. 4:17.

p. 22— "It's not . . . healing process." T. Lashnits, *Maya Lin*, p. 50.

Chapter Three

p. 25— "Absolutely . . . monument designer." B. Moyers interview, "Becoming American." 2003.

p. 26— "I knew . . . to me in school." *Boundaries*, p. 4:26.

p. 26–27— "I realized . . . was about . . . about water." *Boundaries*, p. 4:27.

p. 27— "I am conveying . . . or equal." *Boundaries*, p. 4:28.

p. 30— "I wanted . . . and-effect relationship." *Boundaries*, p. 4:28.

p. 33— "I wanted . . . come alive." F. L. Mock. *Maya Lin: A Strong Clear Vision*, DVD. 1994.

Chapter Four

p. 35— "A strong . . . my work." *Boundaries*, p. 2:07.

p. 35— "It started . . . of a lizard." *Boundaries*, p. 6:04.

p. 35— "When I . . . sculpting the earth." Author interview with Maya Lin, June 17, 2014.

p. 36— "Each project . . . new subject." *Boundaries*, p. 3:07.

p. 36— "The image . . . looking for." *Boundaries*, p. 6:18.

p. 38— "I spent . . . isn't one." *Boundaries*, p. 6:21.

p. 38— "I physically . . . wave form." *Boundaries*, p. 6:21.

p. 38–41— "Its scale . . . you like." *Boundaries*, p. 6:21.

p. 43— "It is . . . disconcerting." R. Andrews, *Maya Lin: Storm King Wavefield*, p. 9.

p. 44— "What I'm . . . in nature." T. Lashnits, *Maya Lin*, p. 75.

Chapter Five

p. 48— "I'd never . . . save it." C. Kreyling, "Lin Finds New Use for Old Barn." May 2000.

p. 48— "The idea . . . inner layer." *Boundaries*, p. 10:24.

p. 50— "slipped in." *Boundaries*, p. 10:24.

p. 50— "always feel . . . the land." *Boundaries*, p. 10:29.

p. 50— "As you . . . exterior timbers." *Boundaries*, p. 10:24.

p. 50— "marvel of . . . Chinese lantern." R. Hackett, "Maya Lin's Courage." October 19, 2000.

p. 52— "The night . . . my people." L. Hughes, *The Collected Poems*, p. 36.

p. 54— "I do . . . at once." Author interview with Maya Lin, June 17, 2014.

p. 54— "My love . . . making things again." J. G. Castro, "One Who Sees Space." September 2002.

p. 57— "to carry . . . safe harbor." H. J. Spica, "Maya Lin launches good month for Design Lab." August 5, 2004.

p. 57— "My goal . . . beautiful surroundings." H. J. Spica, "Maya Lin launches good month for Design Lab." August 5, 2004.

Chapter Six

p. 59— "What were you talking about?" Academy of Achievement, "Maya Lin: Artist and Architect." June 16, 2000.

p. 59-60— "All the . . . very determined." T. Lashnits, *Maya Lin*, p. 57.

p. 60— "She worked . . . of us." T. Lashnits, *Maya Lin*, p. 60.

p. 60— "It was . . . this place." T. Lashnits, *Maya Lin*, p. 66.

p. 61— "There was . . . come from." J. Davidson, "Maya Lin's Big Dig," August 24, 2009.

p. 63— "It's been . . . can land." Author's notes in MOCA.

p. 64— "The building . . . harvested woods." M. Cohen, "The Collector." March 29, 2010.

p. 67— "I think . . . are present." Maya Lin's plaque at MOCA.

Chapter Seven

p. 69— "Absolutely . . . Confluence people?" Author interview with Maya Lin, June 17, 2014.

p. 69— "I'm not . . . monument business." J. Guilbert, "Reversing Course." November 2008.

p. 70— "Lewis and . . . delve deeper." Author interview with Maya Lin, June 17, 2014.

p. 71— "Each one . . . the sea." Author interview with Maya Lin, June 17, 2014.

p. 71— "holding up . . . Clark's journey." "Maya Lin and the Confluence Project," OPB, November 11, 2010.

p. 71— "A lot . . . was here." J. Guilbert, "Reversing Course." November 2008.

p. 74— "It's also . . . men came." M. Parfit, "35 Who Made a Difference: Maya Lin." November 2005.

p. 74— "beeline to the ocean." Author interview with Maya Lin, June 17, 2014.

p. 77— "Saw several . . . the joy." Clark's journal, Lewis and Clark Interpretive Center State Park.

p. 77— "We call . . . us the way." Lewis and Clark Interpretive Center State Park.

Chapter Eight

p. 79— "I can't . . . many projects." Author interview with Maya Lin, June 17, 2014.

p. 79— "I love . . . Box House." Author interview with Maya Lin, June 17, 2014.

p. 80— "We asked Maya . . . destroy it." E. Covington, "Box House on the Mesa." Summer 2007.

p. 80— "I love . . . outdoor rooms." Author interview with Maya Lin, June 17, 2014.

p. 80— "The design . . . secretive element." *Boundaries*, p. 10:23.

p. 80— "I wanted . . . could change." *Boundaries*, p. 10:16.

p. 80— "I think . . . the space." *Boundaries*, p. 10:04.

p. 80— "The Box . . . quite playful." S. Amelar, "Inspired by Asian Puzzle Toys." April 2006.

Chapter Nine

p. 85— "What can . . . closer attention." Author interview with Maya Lin, June 17, 2014.

p. 86-88— "all it . . . set free." M. Thomas, "Maya Lin invites and challenges visitors." April 18, 2012.

p. 88— "Together we . . . one tree." A. Reed, "What Is Missing?" October 12, 2010.

p. 90— "We can't . . . better future?" P. Leonard, "Maya Lin's 'Sound Ring' unveiled at Lab of Ornithology." June 3, 2014.

p. 90— "There's a . . . a difference." Author interview with Maya Lin, June 17, 2014.

p. 91— "It's my . . . can heal." Author interview with Maya Lin, June 17, 2014.

IMAGE CREDITS

INDEX